*The
Gandhi
Nobody
Knows*

The Gandhi Nobody Knows

Richard Grenier

Thomas Nelson Publishers
Nashville • Camden • New York

For Norman and Midge

Published in Nashville, Tennessee, by Thomas
Nelson, Inc. and distributed in Canada by
Lawson Falle, Ltd., Cambridge, Ontario.

Printed in the United States of America.

ISBN 0-8407-5871-5

Cover design by Cioni Artworks / Mark Duebner

Foreword

It seems we live in a day of selective skepticism. Our supposedly cynical, hardbitten media prides itself on "Watergate type" journalistic exposes, in which all subterfuge and hypocrisies are revealed. But it often turns out that this approach is far from even-handed and sometimes deliberately arbitrary.

Since Gandhi was a 20th century figure, and presumably journalists are free to travel to the continent of India, one could assume that in the spirit of investigative reporting the reviews of the film *Gandhi* would be balanced by some historical "fact finding" about the film's accuracy in its "historical" portrayal of the man. One would also assume that the behavior of

The Gandhi Nobody Knows

India as a nation, in living up to Gandhi's alleged dreams, (peace, brotherhood, nonviolence), would be compared to the realities of present-day India. But this has not been the case. Much of the coverage of Gandhi—the film and the man—India, and the religion of Hinduism, has moved to a plateau that can only be called propaganda.

For those of us who dislike instant human deities, (one nice lady told me after seeing the film, "Gandhi was another Jesus!"), Richard Grenier's book is particularly welcome, since it thoroughly pops this wide-eyed bubble. Grenier writes with wit and humor in addition to historic accuracy. But the importance of this book is much more than just an exercise in bubble popping.

To me as a Christian, this is a tremendously important work because of the fact that there are two ways that Christ's unique person can be destroyed in the minds of human beings. The first and more usual way is simply to "debunk" the religious truths of the Bible and the person of Christ. But the second way is perhaps more insidious, though less obvious; this is to elevate other persons, mere mortals, to Christlike status and speak of them with the same reverence normally attributed to our worship of God.

In the film *Gandhi* and much of the mythology surrounding him today, Gandhi has been, in effect, elevated to something approaching western man's idea of sainthood. I could understand the rather breathless adulation of Gandhi by the lady I mentioned earlier, but supposedly more informed people have also, it seems, fallen prey to the pro-Gandhi-what-can-the-decadent-West-learn-from-the-idealist-East propaganda surrounding the release of the Gandhi film. For instance, *Christianity Today* magazine ran a cover story recently titled, "Learning from Gandhi," and sub-titled "Does Western Christianity Have Anything to Learn from the Hindu Who Learned So Much from Christ?" No doubt for the writer of the piece and the magazine it was a pleasant experience to appear so fashionably "with it," but such accolades to Gandhi, particularly in the Christian community, seem a little misplaced, especially when one considers that magazines such as *Christianity Today* regularly contain advertisements for organizations raising funds to feed the starving population of the nation that was founded by "the Hindu who learned so much from Christ." No doubt, that grass always appears greener on the other side of the fence is one explanation of articles that purport to help us "learn from Gandhi." There are undoubtedly regions of the world from which we do indeed have something to learn, but India? Hinduism?

The elevation of Gandhi to near sainthood is an unhappy occurrence for several reasons. First, it devaluates the currency of true worship and true divinity. Second, it has, in the case of Gandhi, the unhappy by-product of leading people astray into taking much more seriously than they should an historical figure who had more than his share of human failings (as you shall see when you read this book).

Christians and others must realize that there are vast distinctions between Hinduism and Christianity. Even more important, we must realize that there are even larger differences in the *results* that the two religious systems bring. Judaism and Christianity have produced cultures in which the concepts of individual dignity and worth, including the sanctity of life, have been produced and preserved in a way that Hindu culture has never known.

There is the matter of fantasy versus reality here. In the world of fantasy, India is a peace-loving country full of gentle, loving, vegetarian pacifists who go about their daily business in a way that should make those of us who are westerners humble and willing to "learn from them." In the world of reality, India is a country in which violent bloodshed is commonplace, wars with neighboring countries—Pakistan, China—are routine,

The Gandhi Nobody Knows

the atom bomb has been tested and
exploded, and rival Hindu and Muslim
tribes hack at each other with farming
implements, paying special attention to
killing women and children. It is time that
westerners—Christians and Jews—adopt a
little more self-confidence in answering the
challenge of Hinduism. Christians in
particular need to reaffirm the fact that
there is only one Christ and Savior and his
name is Jesus, not Gandhi.

Franky A. Schaeffer
April, 1983

Introduction

The reader, I think, has the right to know something about me. I appear to have been born (primitive and vulgar though this has been made to seem in subsequent decades) extremely patriotic. Both my paternal and maternal grandparents, who came from very different parts of the world, were the kind of people so proud to become Americans that they framed their Certificates of Naturalization and hung them on the wall. They learned English eagerly, and spoke it willingly to their children. They never felt the slightest desire ever to visit the countries where they had been born. When they came to America it had been, they knew, for a reason. They felt it to be a freer, better land than the places they had come from. They threw in their lot, forever, with this new people. They pledged their allegiance to the Stars and Stripes with all their hearts. They were Americans. For some reason, this has never left me.

I am a graduate of the U.S. Naval Academy. After the Navy I studied at Harvard, became a Fulbright Scholar, and studied further at the Sorbonne and the Institute of Political Studies in Paris. Somehow, the smattering of education that has come my way has never estranged me from the traditional values of my homeland—an estrangement that seems to be the lot of so many people who enter the "intellectual" class. I have earned my living as a newsman for the French, British, and American press, and have spent most of my life visiting and reporting on much of the world. What my opinions of this outside world would be if I had remained in my native Boston, I cannot know. My personal oddity is that I have been possessed of a peculiarly intense curiosity and a seemingly unquenchable wanderlust. I have seen a great deal of the world, have read omnivorously, and, perhaps in consequence, when ecstatic enthusiasms have broken out in America for alien cultures, exalted, more noble ways of organizing society, or exotic religions, I have proved singularly immune to their enchantment.

I at no time, for even the blink of an eye, have ever admired Moscow, Havana, or Hanoi. I have been given the red carpet treatment in totalitarian countries, been fed caviar and driven about in luxurious government limousines, but for some reason it has never taken. I have also been treated less ceremoniously, being arrested by Soviet paratroopers during the Soviet invasion of Prague in 1968. But for all the courtesy shown me by these paratroopers (not shooting me, for example), and despite unrelenting efforts on my part to keep my mind open, I have found all the societies I have visited frankly inferior to our own. It has been pointed out to me that I have never visited Albania, however (one of the few countries in Eastern or Western

The Gandhi Nobody Knows

Europe I have *not* visited), so perhaps I still have a revelation in store.

The estrangement from the values of our society that has possessed our intellectual class is too complex a matter to be pondered here. But one of the seemingly necessary concomitants of such an alienation has always been the systematic offering of exemplary, alternative societies—societies better, that is to say, than our own. Depending on the whimsy of the speaker, they may have more just, equitable, and humane values than ours, more sense of community, more unity of purpose, more "authenticity" (Southeast Asia was a wonderful example of this until a Gulag system was established in Vietnam and some millions of Cambodians were slaughtered by Pol Pot). Or, in turn, it might be their *spiritual* values that are more profound: here India, for several decades now, has had pride of place. Professors of comparative religion are frequently in a positive ecstasy about Hinduism, although, oddly, they almost never mention to their students the distressing subject of caste—the flagrantly undemocratic and inhumane pillar on which all Hindu society rests. Such professors, of course, take a detached view of all religions (otherwise how could they analyze them dispassionately?), and you can see why the horrors of the caste system would cause them some embarrassment. An affirmation that Judeo-Christian society was categorically superior even on ethical grounds, moreover, might positively put them out of business.

You hear bizarre and wonderful things if you live in the intellectual world. At the time of the Jaruzelski crackdown in Poland, while at the home of a senior official of the National Endowment for the Arts, I heard an extremely bellicose man proclaim that President Reagan was at least as bad as Jaruzelski, that he would proclaim martial law, and that we would soon see tanks patrolling the streets in New York City. Not long afterward an extremely celebrated intellectual lady— after long years of eminence, at last, I hope, going into a decline—assured me with great conviction that socialism "really works" in North Korea. And shortly after that, at still another Manhattan party, where I freely granted the highly imperfect nature of our own society, I asked an interlocutor to offer an example of a better one somewhere, just to set a standard of comparison. The answer was "Angola." Now you will notice no stream of intellectuals leaving the United States for either Angola or North Korea. And, unless I have been extremely unobservant, there have been no tanks patrolling the streets of New York City. But I should doubt very much if any of these people have altered their fundamental opinions in consequence.

One of the marks of our age, whether caused by the decline of religious faith, the pathology of affluence, or whatever, is that the grip on reality of the intellectual and artistic classes has become extremely intermittent—a trait now spread among extensive and influential sections of the population. The withdrawal from a society of its absolute and sublime values (the

traditional custodian of which was
religion) has set vast numbers of people
quite adrift, feckless, reckless,
irresponsible. It is perhaps not entirely
accidental that none of the people I quoted
above has any religious faith, and one of
them, the "celebrated intellectual lady,"
has a hostility to religion of a rare
ferocity—leaving her, from the evidence,
wide open to any snake-oil salesman
promising a secular paradise. But
Hinduism does not promise a secular
paradise. And the history of Hindophilia,
and Gandhi-ophilia, in the United States
has a history of its own.

As World War II drew to a close, and it
was not yet apparent to Washington that
territories being overrun by the Red Army
were destined for decades, if not
generations, of Soviet rule, a delegation of
scholars of Communism and the Soviet
Union conferred with President Harry
Truman. The President told them, to their
horror, that he felt the greatest threat to
freedom in the world of that time was the

British Empire. The succeeding years, with the blockade of Berlin, the Prague coup, and the Korean War, taught President Truman some sobering lessons. But his earlier attitude was typical of a significant side current of the pre-War period. And of course the greatest hero of the struggle against this evil British Empire was Mahatma Gandhi. His assassination by a religious fanatic in 1948 for all practical purposes canonized him. Until the extremely recent 1980s "peace" movement, therefore, the great burst of Gandhi idolatry was confined almost entirely to this earlier period, with Gandhi the hero of anti-colonialism, and then a martyr to religious tolerance. The Gandhi legend was heavily falsified even then, mind you. But I should make clear, in defense of Gandhi's admirers of that period, that World War II, and the years that both preceded and followed it, were terrible times. Gandhi was a man of a markedly tyrannical temperament, but compared to the other tyrants of the era—which is to say, Hitler and Stalin—he was really quite a splendid fellow. Of this let there be no doubt. The times, as I say, were quite gruesome, and they help explain the quite extraordinary fervor that Gandhi once awakened in the West.

Then followed a very interesting period, now almost as completely gone as the British Empire, but which for some decades saved Gandhi and the newly independent India from the dread rigors of revisionism. In the early 50s the West and the Soviet bloc were at swords' points in Europe, but also, simultaneously, if by less direct means, the battle was on for Asia. The world's two most populous countries by far were Asian: China and India. China, at the time, was a totalitarian state seemingly on the Soviet model and a loyal ally of Moscow, while India, after all, had a variety of parties, a free press. The most fanciful notions were encouraged during the period as to the democratic nature of India. President Eisenhower loved India. Henry Luce loved India. Chester Bowles (not an advertising millionaire for nothing) loved India with a passion. India was our candidate in the great Asian Sweepstakes, and we were not about to look a gift Hindu in the mouth.

The spectacular break between Moscow and Peking in the early 60s set the stage for President Nixon's "opening to China" a decade later, which opening put us on friendly terms with Pakistan, a country India hates even more than it hates China—and the whole "Battle for Asia" was turned on its head. We now, with jarring ups and downs, have some sort of modus vivendi with China, sharing, as we do, a joint antagonist in the Soviet Union. India, on the other hand, roughly speaking, has become a client state of Moscow, rendering it services in all international forums. And yet for most Americans, India remains, in V. S. Naipaul's phrase, "an area of darkness." Since India stopped being our candidate in the Great Asian Sweepstakes, Americans have rarely given India a thought, still retaining—though Hindus are butchering thousands of Muslim refugees from Bangladesh even as I write—a vague feeling of piety for this peace-loving people.

So when Indians, doing their utmost to foster the new wave of pacifism in the West (one does what one can for one's friends), converted Gandhi, the father of their country, into a kind of Saint Francis of Assisi, Americans swallowed it whole. At least, American film critics swallowed it whole, as did Hollywood's Academy of Motion Picture Arts and Sciences, granting it eight 1983 Academy Awards. Martin Sheen, the star of *Apocalypse Now*, who plays the "American journalist" in *Gandhi*, said it "brought me back to Catholicism"— which, since Gandhi was a Hindu, will bring neither the movie nor Mr. Sheen any prizes for doctrinal purity. Then again, perhaps Mr. Sheen has become the kind of new Catholic who, like Archbishop Hunthausen of Seattle, thinks our nuclear submarine base in that archdiocese is "the Auschwitz of Puget Sound." By extension, of course, this is what *Gandhi* is about. Unlike its eponymous hero, who was no pacifist by any manner of means, the film *Gandhi* is straight pacifist disinformation.

And yet there is light. Before the publication of the magazine article that was the germ of the present book, it was widely predicted that I would be fallen upon like some kind of monster, a destroyer of all that is good and beautiful. But I marshalled my facts and stood my ground. The article did, I grant, produce something of an explosion. But a blizzard of mail, and a typhoon of telephone calls, have been running twenty to one in my favor. The *Chicago Sun-Times* excerpted five thousand words from the article, with which they led their Sunday feature section. The *Los Angeles Herald-Examiner* did the same. The *Dallas Morning News* and the *Milwaukee Sentinel* ran editorials in my support. I was invited to speak on numerous talk shows. A Hindu with whom I debated deferred to my scholarship right along the line, hoping only that I would admit that Gandhi was holy, which, since he was a Hindu, I

The Gandhi Nobody Knows

generously allowed him. As far as Harvard is concerned these days I consider myself a bit of a renegade, so I was perhaps most surprised to hear that the *Harvard Crimson,* too, had enrolled beneath my banners. I confess, when you have read the facts about Gandhi, that they are pretty hard to argue with. But I am slightly appalled that of millions of Americans, facing a media blitz portraying an entirely bogus version of one of the most famous men in modern history, I was one of only two driven to set the record straight. The other was Elliott Stein writing, of all places, in *The Village Voice.*

Anyone who has worked on a newspaper or opinion journal knows that people write letters to the editor more out of rage than contentment. But, in this case, they were far more outraged at Sir Richard Attenborough than they were at me. In fact, hardly anyone was outraged at me. A few gallant souls leaped to the defense of the beauteous Candice Bergen, to whom, they said, I was disrespectful. But for a man who likes a good debate, I am saddened to report that the handful of hostile letters I received made a pretty pathetic showing: illiterate (many misspellings), wild, sometimes with a hint of madness, hopelessly irrational. I had taken away their "Gandhi"—a character they seemed to picture as a kind of Asian E.T.—and this left them in a state of unattractive venomousness.

One gentleman was incensed that I had criticized Gandhi for suggesting that the Jews deal with the Nazi threat by committing collective suicide. Collective suicide for Jews would have been a splendid idea, he thought. Another was quite furious at my recalling "all the ugly details of the caste system," and accused me of a "base appeal to religious prejudice." A letter on the stationery of the Political Science Department of the University of Cincinnati was one of the more rabid, and the worst spelled. Addressing me repeatedly as "Mr. Greiner" (transposing a French name into a German one, which disturbs me not in the slightest but makes me wonder how carefully he read my article), the author seemed utterly convinced that, properly applied, Gandhi's techniques of non-violent resistance would have worked very effectively against Hitler's S.S. Since this letter-writer is pretty close to being in a minority of one, I would prefer to think, all things considered, that people have been stealing stationery from the Political Science Department of the University of Cincinnati.

An accusation leveled at me with particular resentment was that I had been "scatalogical" in noting Gandhi's preoccupation with enemas and excrement and the Hindu "deification of filth" (a phrase of Naipaul's, incidentally). But I did not *invent* Gandhi's preoccupation with enemas and excrement—about which he talked and wrote endlessly. I merely recorded it, since it occupied such a large part of his thinking and was strictly germane to my comments on Hinduism. It is not my fault if devout Hindus, in pursuit of sanctity, daily drink a glass of their own urine. It is not my fault if Hindus eat cow dung (on special occasions). It is not my fault if Hindus are among the most bestially violent people on the face of the globe. If you do not know these things about Hindus, and about Gandhi, you do not really know much about India. You have been getting your information from pacifists and Gandhi groupies, who have been keeping you in a state of retarded innocence.

I shall not quote the many complimentary letters I received, a significant portion of which tended to run, "How *dare* that Attenborough. . . ." One of the most interesting letters, however, recalled Gandhi's words on the subject of the new "atomic bomb" to Margaret Bourke-White, the *Life* photographer, the last person to interview him before his assassination. Gandhi would meet the atomic bomb, he said, with "prayerful action." "I will not go underground," he announced. "I will not go into shelters. I will come out in the open and let the pilot see I have not the face of evil against him. The pilot will not see our faces from his

great height, I know, but the longing in our
hearts that he will not come to harm
would reach up to him and his eyes would
be opened."

Since India is now a nuclear power such
reflections could have no place in
Attenborough's movie, of course, but this is
regrettable, in a way, because they clearly
contain the core of a remarkably
inexpensive ABM system, which, since it
doesn't depend on optical contact, would
still be available to us today. If we all just
stood out in the open and longed in our
hearts that no harm would come to the
officers in the Soviet missile silos, then
this longing would reach out to them and
their eyes would be opened. One of
Gandhi's most extraordinary qualities,
furthermore, as you will see in this book, is
his capacity for instant self-contradiction.
The sentence of Gandhi I quoted above
promises quite clearly that if we longed
properly in our hearts the eyes of our
adversaries "would be opened." But in the
very next sentence Gandhi rambled off
about how much better the world would be

if the thousands who died at Hiroshima had perished with just such a longing, "if they had died with that prayerful action— died openly with that prayer in their hearts. . . ." In short, all that longing is no protection against incineration after all. One second we are promised that prayerful action will open our enemy's eyes, the next that it will guarantee us martyrdom. The reader can see why I am reluctant to accept lessons in conduct from Mr. Gandhi.

*The
Gandhi
Nobody
Knows*

I had the singular honor of attending an early private screening of *Gandhi* with an audience of invited guests from the National Council of Churches. At the end of the three-hour movie there was hardly, as they say, a dry eye in the house. When the lights came up I fell into conversation with a young woman who observed, reverently, that Gandhi's last words were "Oh, God," causing me to remark regretfully that the real Gandhi had not spoken in English, but had cried, *Hai Rama!* ("Oh, Rama"). Well, Rama was just Indian for God, she replied, at which I felt compelled to explain that, alas, Rama, collectively with his three half-brothers, represented the seventh reincarnation of

Vishnu. The young woman, who seemed to have been under the impression that Hinduism was Christianity under another name, sensed somehow that she had fallen on an uncongenial spirit, and the conversation ended.

At a dinner party shortly afterward, a friend of mine, who had visited India many times and even gone to the trouble of learning Hindi, objected strenuously that the picture of Gandhi that emerges in the movie is grossly inaccurate, omitting, as one of many examples, that when Gandhi's wife lay dying of pneumonia and British doctors insisted that a shot of penicillin would save her, Gandhi refused to have this alien medicine injected in her body and simply let her die. (It must be noted that when Gandhi contracted malaria shortly afterward he accepted for himself the alien medicine quinine, and that when he had appendicitis he allowed British doctors to perform on him the alien outrage of an appendectomy.) All of this produced a wistful mooing from an editor of a major newspaper and a recalcitrant,

The Gandhi Nobody Knows

"But still. . . ." I would prefer to explicate things more substantial than a wistful mooing, but there is little doubt it meant the editor in question felt that even if the real Mohandas K. Gandhi had been different from the Gandhi of the movie it would have been *nice* if he had been like the movie-Gandhi, and that presenting him in this admittedly false manner was beautiful, stirring, and perhaps socially beneficial.

An important step in the canonization of this movie-Gandhi was taken by the New York Film Critics Circle, which not only awarded the picture its prize as best film of 1982, but awarded Ben Kingsley, who played Gandhi (a remarkably good performance), its prize as best actor of the year. But I cannot believe for one second that these awards were made independently of the film's content— which, not to put too fine a point on it, is an all-out appeal for pacifism—or in anything but the most shameful ignorance of the historical Gandhi.

Now it does not bother me that

The Gandhi Nobody Knows

Shakespeare omitted from his *King John* the signing of the Magna Charta—by far the most important event in John's reign. All Shakespeare's "histories" are strewn with errors and inventions. Shifting to the cinema and to more recent times, it is hard for me to work up much indignation over the fact that neither Eisenstein's *Battleship Potemkin* nor his *October* recounts historical episodes in anything like the manner in which they actually occurred (the famous march of the White Guards down the steps at Odessa—artistically one of the greatest sequences in film history— simply did not take place). As we draw closer to the present, however, the problem becomes much more difficult. If the Soviet Union were to make an artistically wondrous film about the entry of Russian tanks into Prague in 1968 (an event I happened to witness), and show them being greeted with flowers by a grateful populace, the Czechs dancing in the streets with joy, I do not guarantee that I would maintain my serene aloofness. A great deal depends on whether the historical events represented in a movie are intended to be taken as substantially true, and also on whether—separated from us by some decades or occurring yesterday—they are seen as having a direct bearing on courses of action now open to us.

On my second viewing of *Gandhi*, this time at a public showing at the end of the Christmas season, I happened to leave the theater behind three teenage girls, apparently from one of Manhattan's fashionable private schools. "Gandhi was pretty much an FDR," one opined, astonishing me almost as much by her breezy use of initials to invoke a President who died almost a quarter-century before her birth as by the stupefying nature of the comparison. "But he was a religious figure, too," corrected one of her friends, adding somewhat smugly, "It's not in our historical tradition to honor spiritual leaders." Since her schoolteachers had clearly not led her to consider Jonathan Edwards and Roger Williams as spiritual leaders, let alone Joseph Smith and William Jennings Bryan, the intimation seemed to be that we are a society with poorer spiritual values than, let's say, India. There can be no question, in any event, that the girls felt they had just been shown the historical Gandhi—an attitude shared by Ralph Nader, who at last account had seen the film three times. Nader has conceived the most extraordinary notion that Gandhi's symbolic flouting of the British salt tax was a "consumer issue" which he later expanded into the wider one of Indian independence. A modern parallel to Gandhi's program of home-spinning and home-weaving, another "consumer issue" says Nader, might be the use of solar energy to free us from the "giant multinational oil corporations."

As IT happens, the government of India openly admits to having provided one-third of the financing of *Gandhi* out of state funds, straight out of the national treasury—and after close study of the finished product I would not be a bit surprised to hear that it was one hundred percent. If Pandit Nehru is portrayed flatteringly in the film, one must remember that Nehru himself took part in the initial story conferences (he originally wanted Gandhi to be played by Alec Guinness) and that his daughter Indira Gandhi is, after all, Prime Minister of India (though no relation to Mohandas Gandhi). The screenplay was checked and rechecked by Indian officials at every stage, often by the Prime Minister herself, with close consultations on plot and even casting. If the movie contains a particularly poisonous portrait of Mohammed Ali Jinnah, the founder of Pakistan, the Indian reply, I suppose, would be that if the Pakistanis want an attractive portrayal of Jinnah let them pay for their own movie. A friend of mine, highly sophisticated in political matters but innocent about film-making, declared that *Gandhi* should be preceded by the legend: *The following film is a paid political advertisement by the government of India.*

 Gandhi, then, is a large, pious, historical morality tale centered on a saintly,

The Gandhi Nobody Knows

sanitized Mahatma Gandhi cleansed of anything too embarrassingly Hindu (the word "caste" is not mentioned from one end of the film to the other) and, indeed, of most of the rest of Gandhi's life, much of which would drastically diminish his saintliness in Western eyes. There is little to indicate that the India of today has followed Gandhi's precepts in almost nothing. There is little, in fact, to indicate that India is even India. The spectator realizes the scene is the Indian subcontinent because there are thousands of extras dressed in dhotis and saris. The characters go about talking in these quaint Peter Sellers accents. We have occasional shots of India's holy poverty, holy hovels, some landscapes, many of them photographed quite beautifully, for those who like travelogues. We have a character called Lord Mountbatten (India's last Viceroy); a composite American journalist (assembled from Vincent Sheean, William L. Shirer, Louis Fischer, and straight fiction); a character called simply "Viceroy" (presumably another composite);

an assemblage of Gandhi's Indian followers under the name of one of them (Patel); and of course Nehru.

I sorely missed the fabulous Annie Besant, that English clergyman's wife, turned atheist, turned Theosophist, turned Indian nationalist, who actually became president of the Indian National Congress and had a terrific falling out with Gandhi, becoming his fierce opponent. And if the producers felt they had to work in a cameo role for an American star to add to the film's appeal in the United States, it is positively embarrassing that they should have brought in the photographer Margaret Bourke-White, a person of no importance whatever in Gandhi's life and a role Candice Bergen plays with a repellant unctuousness. If the film-makers had been interested in drama and not hagiography, it is hard to see how they could have resisted the awesome confrontation between Gandhi and, yes, Margaret Sanger. For the two did meet. Now *there* was a meeting of East and West, and *may the better person win!* (She did. Margaret Sanger argued her views on birth control with such vigor that Gandhi had a nervous breakdown.)

I cannot honestly say I had any reasonable expectation that the film would show scenes of Gandhi's pretty teenage girl followers fighting "hysterically" (the word was used) for the honor of sleeping naked with the Mahatma and cuddling the nude septuagenarian in their arms. (Gandhi was "testing" his vow of chastity in order to gain moral strength for his mighty struggle with Jinnah.) When told there was a man named Freud who said that, despite his declared intention, Gandhi might actually be *enjoying* the caresses of the naked girls, Gandhi continued, unperturbed. Nor, frankly, did I expect to see Gandhi giving daily enemas to all the young girls in his ashrams (his daily greeting was, "Have you had a good bowel movement this morning, sisters?"), nor see the girls giving him *his* daily enema. Although Gandhi seems to have written less about home rule for India than he did about enemas, and excrement, and latrine cleaning ("The bathroom is a temple. It should be so clean and inviting that anyone would enjoy eating there"), I confess such scenes might pose problems for a Western director.

Gandhi, therefore, the film, this paid political advertisement for the government of India, is organized around three axes: (1) Anti-racism—all men are equal regardless of race, color, creed, etc.; (2) anti-colonialism, which in present terms translates as support for the Third World, including, most eminently, India; (3) nonviolence, presented as an absolutist pacifism. There are other, secondary precepts and subheadings. Gandhi is portrayed as the quintessence of tolerance ("I am a Hindu and a Muslim and a Christian and a Jew"), of basic friendliness to Britain ("The British have been with us for a long time and when they leave we want them to leave as friends"), of devotion to his wife and family. His vow of chastity is represented as something selfless and holy, rather like the celibacy of the Catholic clergy. But, above all, Gandhi's life and teachings are presented as having

great import for us today. We must learn
from Gandhi.

I propose to demonstrate that the film
grotesquely distorts both Gandhi's life and
character to the point that it is nothing
more than a pious fraud, and a fraud of
the most egregious kind. Hackneyed Indian
falsehoods such as that "the British keep
trying to break India up" (as if Britain
didn't give India a unity it had never
enjoyed in history), or that the British
created Indian poverty (a poverty which
had not only existed since time
immemorial but had been considered holy),
almost pass unnoticed in the tide of
adulation for our fictional saint. Gandhi,
admittedly, being a devout Hindu, was far
more self-contradictory than most public
men. Sanskrit scholars tell me that flat
self-contradiction is even considered an
element of "Sanskrit rhetoric." Perhaps it
is thought to show profundity.

GANDHI rose early, usually at three-thirty,
and before his first bowel movement
(during which he received visitors,

44

although possibly not Margaret Bourke-White) he spent two hours in meditation, listening to his "inner voice." Now Gandhi was an extremely vocal individual, and in addition to spending an hour each day in vigorous walking, another hour spinning at his primitive spinning wheel, another hour at further prayers, another hour being massaged nude by teenage girls, and many hours deciding such things as affairs of state, he produced a quite unconscionable number of articles and speeches and wrote an average of sixty letters a day. All considered, it is not really surprising that his inner voice said different things to him at different times. Despising consistency and never checking his earlier statements, and yet inhumanly obstinate about his position at any given moment, Gandhi is thought by some Indians today (according to V. S. Naipaul) to have been so erratic and unpredictable that he may have delayed Indian independence for twenty-five years.

For Gandhi was an extremely difficult man to work with. He had no partners, only disciples. For members of his ashrams, he dictated every minute of their days, and not only every morsel of food they should eat but when they should eat it. Without ever having heard of a protein or a vitamin, he considered himself an expert on diet, as on most things, and was constantly experimenting. Once when he fell ill, he was found to have been living on a diet of ground-nut butter and lemon juice; British doctors called it malnutrition. And Gandhi had even greater confidence in his abilities as a "nature doctor," prescribing obligatory cures for his ashramites, such as dried cow-dung powder and various concoctions containing cow dung (the cow, of course, being sacred to the Hindu). And to those he really loved he gave enemas—but again, alas, not to Margaret Bourke-White. Which is too bad, really. For admiring Candice Bergen's work as I do, I would have been most interested in seeing how she would have experienced this beatitude. The scene might have lived in film history.

There are four hundred biographies of

The Gandhi Nobody Knows

Gandhi, and his writings run to eighty volumes, and since he lived to be seventy-nine, and rarely fell silent, there are, as I have indicated, quite a few inconsistencies. The authors of the present movie even acknowledge in a little-noticed opening title that they have made a film only true to Gandhi's "spirit." For my part, I do not intend to pick through Gandhi's writings to make him look like Attila the Hun (although the thought is tempting), but to give a fair, weighted balance of his views, laying stress above all on his actions, and on what he told other men to do when the time for action had come.

ANTI-RACISM. The reader will have noticed
that in the present-day community of
nations South Africa is a pariah. So it is
an absolutely amazing piece of good
fortune that Gandhi, born the son of the
Prime Minister of a tiny Indian
principality and received as an attorney at
the bar of the Middle Temple in London,
should have begun his climb to greatness
as a member of the small Indian
community in, precisely, South Africa.
Natal, then a separate colony, wanted to
limit Indian immigration and, as part of
the government program, ordered Indians
to carry identity papers (an action not
without similarities to measures under
consideration in the U.S. today to control

illegal immigration). The film's lengthy opening sequences are devoted to Gandhi's leadership in the fight against Indians carrying their identity papers (burning their registration cards), with for good measure Gandhi being expelled from the first-class section of a railway train, and Gandhi being asked by whites to step off the sidewalk. This inspired young Indian leader calls, in the film, for interracial harmony, for people to "live together."

Now the time is 1893, and Gandhi is a "caste" Hindu, and from one of the higher castes. Although, later, he was to call for improving the lot of India's Untouchables, he was not to have any serious misgivings about the fundamentals of the caste system for about another thirty years, and even then his doubts, to my way of thinking, were rather minor. In the India in which Gandhi grew up, and had only recently left, some castes could enter the courtyards of certain Hindu temples, while others could not. Some castes were forbidden to use the village well. Others were compelled to live outside the village, still others to

leave the road at the approach of a person
of higher caste and perpetually to call out,
giving warning, so that no one would be
polluted by their proximity. The endless
intricacies of Hindu caste by-laws varied
somewhat region by region, but in Madras,
where most South African Indians were
from, while a Nayar could pollute a man of
higher caste only by touching him,
Kammalans polluted at a distance of
twenty-four feet, toddy drawers at thirty-
six feet, Pulayans and Cherumans at forty-
eight feet, and beef-eating Paraiyans at
sixty-four feet. All castes and the
thousands of sub-castes were forbidden,
needless to say, to marry, eat, or engage in
social activity with any but members of
their own group. In Gandhi's native
Gujarat a caste Hindu who had been
polluted by touch had to perform extensive
ritual ablutions or purify himself by
drinking a holy beverage composed of
milk, whey, and (what else?) cow dung.

Low-caste Hindus, in short, suffered
humiliations in their native India
compared to which the carrying of identity

cards in South Africa was almost trivial. In fact, Gandhi, to his credit, was to campaign strenuously in his later life for the reduction of caste barriers in India—a campaign almost invisible in the movie, of course, conveyed in only two glancing references, leaving the audience with the officially sponsored if historically astonishing notion that racism was introduced into India by the British. To present the Gandhi of 1893, a conventional caste Hindu, fresh from caste-ridden India where a Paraiyan could pollute at sixty-four feet, as the champion of interracial equalitarianism is one of the most brazen hypocrisies I have ever encountered in a serious movie.

The film, moreover, does not give the slightest hint as to Gandhi's attitude toward blacks, and the viewers of *Gandhi* would naturally suppose that, since the future Great Soul opposed South African discrimination against Indians, he would also oppose South African discrimination against black people. But this is not so. While Gandhi, in South Africa, fought furiously to have Indians recognized as loyal subjects of the British empire, and to have them enjoy the full rights of Englishmen, he had no concern for blacks whatever. In fact, during one of the "Kaffir Wars" he volunteered to organize a brigade of Indians to put down a Zulu rising, and was decorated himself for valor under fire.

For, yes, Gandhi (Sergeant-Major Gandhi) was awarded Victoria's coveted War Medal. Throughout most of his life Gandhi had the most inordinate admiration for British soldiers, their sense of duty, their discipline and stoicism in defeat (a trait he emulated himself). He marveled that they retreated with heads high, like victors. There was even a time in his life when Gandhi, hardly to be distinguished from Kipling's Gunga Din, wanted nothing so much as to be a Soldier of the Queen. Since this is not in keeping with the "spirit" of Gandhi, as decided by Pandit Nehru and Indira Gandhi, it is naturally omitted from the movie.

ANTI-COLONIALISM. As almost always with historical films, even those more honest than *Gandhi*, the historical personage on which the movie is based is not only more complex but more interesting than the character shown on the screen. During his entire South African period, and for some time after, until he was about fifty, Gandhi was nothing more or less than an imperial loyalist, claiming for Indians the rights of Englishmen but unshakably loyal to the crown. He supported the empire ardently in no fewer than three wars: the Boer War, the "Kaffir War," and, with the most extreme zeal, World War I. If Gandhi's mind were of the modern European sort, this would seem to suggest that his later attitude toward Britain was the product of unrequited love: he had wanted to be an Englishman; Britain had rejected him and his people; very well then, they would have their own country. But this would imply a point of "agonizing reappraisal," a moment when Gandhi's most fundamental political beliefs were reexamined and, after the most bitter soul-searching, repudiated. But I have studied the literature and cannot find this moment of bitter soul-searching. Instead, listening to his "inner voice" (which in the case of divines of all countries often speaks in the tones of holy opportunism), Gandhi simply, tranquilly, without announcing any sharp break, set off in a new direction.

It should be understood that it is unlikely Gandhi ever truly conceived of "becoming" an Englishman, first, because he was a Hindu to the marrow of his bones, and also, perhaps, because his democratic instincts were really quite weak. He was a man of the most extreme, autocratic temperament, tyrannical, unyielding even regarding things he knew nothing about, totally intolerant of all opinions but his own. He was, furthermore, in the highest degree reactionary, permitting in India no change in the relationship between the feudal lord and his peasants or servants, the rich and the poor. In his *The Life and Death of Mahatma Gandhi,* the best and least hagiographic of the full-length studies, Robert Payne, although admiring Gandhi greatly, explains Gandhi's "new direction" on his return to India from South Africa as follows:

> He spoke in generalities, but he was searching for a single cause, a single hard-edged task to which he would devote the remaining years of his life. He wanted to repeat his triumph in South Africa on Indian soil. He dreamed of assembling a small army of dedicated men around him, issuing stern commands and leading them to some almost unobtainable goal.

Gandhi, in short, was a leader looking for a cause. He found it, of course, in home rule for India and, ultimately, in independence.

WE ARE therefore presented with the seeming anomaly of a Gandhi who, in Britain when war broke out in August 1914, instantly contacted the War Office, swore that he would stand by England in its hour of need, and created the Indian Volunteer Corps, which he might have commanded if he hadn't fallen ill with pleurisy. In 1915, back in India, he made a memorable speech in Madras in which he proclaimed, "I discovered that the British empire had certain ideals with which I have fallen in love. . . ." In early 1918, as the war in Europe entered its final crisis, he wrote to the Viceroy of India, "I have an idea that if I become your recruiting agent-in-chief, I might rain men upon you," and he proclaimed in a speech in Kheda that the British "love justice; they have shielded men against oppression." Again, he wrote to the Viceroy, "I would make India offer all her able-bodied sons as a sacrifice to the empire at this critical moment. . . ." To some of his pacifist friends, who were horrified, Gandhi replied by appealing to the *Bhagavad Gita* and to the endless wars recounted in the Hindu epics, the *Ramayana* and the *Mahabharata,* adding further to the pacifists' horror by declaring that Indians "have always been warlike, and the finest hymn composed by Tulsidas in praise of Rama gives the first place to his ability to strike down the enemy."

This was in contradiction to the interpretation of sacred Hindu scriptures Gandhi had offered on earlier occasions (and would offer later), which was that they did not recount military struggles but spiritual struggles; but, unusual for him, he strove to find some kind of synthesis. "I do not say, 'Let us go and kill the Germans,'" Gandhi explained. "I say, 'Let us go and die for the sake of India and the empire.'" And yet within two years, the time having come for *swaraj* (home rule), Gandhi's inner voice spoke again, and, the leader having found his cause, Gandhi proclaimed resoundingly: "The British empire today represents Satanism, and they who love God can afford to have no love for Satan."

The idea of *swaraj*, originated by others, crept into Gandhi's mind gradually. With a fair amount of winding about, Gandhi, roughly, passed through three phases. First, he was entirely pro-British, and merely wanted for Indians the rights of Englishmen (as he understood them). Second, he was still pro-British, but with the belief that, having proved their loyalty to the empire, Indians would be granted some degree of *swaraj*. Third, as the home-rule movement gathered momentum, it was the *swaraj*, the whole *swaraj*, and nothing but the *swaraj*, and he turned relentlessly against the crown. The movie to the contrary, he caused the British no end of trouble in their struggles during World War II.

BUT it should not be thought for one second that Gandhi's finally full-blown desire to detach India from the British empire gave him the slightest sympathy with other colonial peoples pursuing similar objectives. Throughout his entire life Gandhi displayed the most spectacular inability to understand or even really take in people unlike himself—a trait which V. S. Naipaul considers specifically Hindu, and I am inclined to agree. Just as Gandhi had been totally unconcerned with the situation of South Africa's blacks (he hardly noticed they were there until they rebelled), so now he was totally unconcerned with other Asians or Africans. In fact, he was adamantly *opposed* to certain Arab movements within the Ottoman empire for reasons of internal Indian politics.

At the close of World War I, the Muslims of India were deeply absorbed in what they called the "Khilafat" movement— "Khilafat" being their corruption of "Caliphate," the Caliph in question being the Ottoman Sultan. In addition to his temporal powers, the Sultan of the Ottoman empire held the spiritual position of Caliph, supreme leader of the world's Muslims and successor to the Prophet Muhammad. At the defeat of the Central

The Gandhi Nobody Knows

Powers (Germany, Austria, Turkey), the
Sultan was a prisoner in his palace in
Constantinople, shorn of his religious as
well as his political authority, and the
Muslims of India were incensed. It so
happened that the former subject peoples
of the Ottoman empire, principally Arabs,
were perfectly happy to be rid of this
Caliph, and even the Turks were glad to be
rid of him, but this made no impression at
all on the Muslims of India, for whom the
issue was essentially a club with which to
beat the British. Until this odd historical
moment, Indian Muslims had felt little real
allegiance to the Ottoman Sultan either,
but now that he had fallen, the British had
done it! The British had taken away their
Khilafat! And one of the most ardent
supporters of this Indian Muslim
movement was the new Hindu leader,
Gandhi.

No one questions that the formative
period for Gandhi as a political leader was
his time in South Africa. Throughout
history Indians, divided into one thousand
five hundred language and dialect groups

(India today has fifteen official languages), had little sense of themselves as a nation. Muslim Indians and Hindu Indians felt about as close as Christians and Moors during their seven hundred years of cohabitation in Spain. In addition to which, the Hindus were divided into thousands of castes and sub-castes, and there were also Parsees, Sikhs, Jains. But in South Africa officials had thrown them all in together, and in the mind of Gandhi (another one of those examples of nationalism being born in exile) grew the idea of India as a nation, and Muslim-Hindu friendship became one of the few positions on which he never really reversed himself. So Gandhi—ignoring Arabs and Turks—became an adamant supporter of the Khilafat movement out of strident Indian nationalism. He had become a national figure in India for having unified thirteen thousand Indians of all faiths in South Africa, and now he was determined to reach new heights by unifying hundreds of millions of Indians of all faiths in India itself. But this nationalism did not please everyone, particularly Tolstoy, who in his last years carried on a curious correspondence with the new Indian leader. For Tolstoy, Gandhi's Indian nationalism "spoils everything."

As for the "anti-colonialism" of the nationalist Indian state since independence, Indira Gandhi, India's present Prime Minister, hears an inner voice of her own, it would appear, and this inner voice told her to justify the Soviet invasion of Afghanistan as produced by provocative maneuvers on the part of the U.S. and China, as well as to be the first country outside the Soviet bloc to recognize the Hanoi puppet regime in Cambodia. So everything plainly depends on who is colonizing whom, and Mrs. Gandhi's voice perhaps tells her that the subjection of Afghanistan and Cambodia to foreign rule is "defensive" colonialism. And the movie's message that Mahatma Gandhi, and by plain implication India (the country for which he plays the role of Joan of Arc), have taken a holy, unchanging stance against the colonization of nation by nation is just another of its hypocrisies. For India, when it comes to colonialism or anti-colonialism, it has been *Realpolitik* all the way.

NONVIOLENCE. But the real center and
raison d'être of *Gandhi* is *ahimsa,*
nonviolence, which principle when
incorporated into vast campaigns of
noncooperation with British rule the
Mahatma called by an odd name he made
up himself, *satyagraha,* which means
something like "truth-striving." During the
key part of his life, Gandhi devoted a great
deal of time explaining the moral and
philosophical meanings of both *ahimsa* and
satyagraha. But much as the film sanitizes
Gandhi to the point where one would
mistake him for a Christian saint, and
sanitizes India to the point where one
would take it for Shangri-la, it quite
sweeps away Gandhi's ethical and religious

ponderings, his complexities, his
qualifications, and certainly his
vacillations, which simplifying process
leaves us with our old European friend:
pacifism. It is true that Gandhi was much
impressed by the Sermon on the Mount,
his favorite passage in the Bible, which he
read over and over again. But for all the
Sermon's inspirational value, and its
service as an ideal in relations among
individual human beings, no Christian
state which survived has ever based its
policies on the Sermon on the Mount since
Constantine declared Christianity the
official religion of the Roman empire. And
no modern Western state which survives
can ever base its policies on pacifism. And
no Hindu state will ever base its policies
on *ahimsa*. Gandhi himself—although the
film dishonestly conceals this from us—
many times conceded that in dire
circumstances "war may have to be
resorted to as a necessary evil."

It is something of an anomaly that
Gandhi, held in popular myth to be a pure
pacifist (a myth which governments of

The Gandhi Nobody Knows

India have always been at great pains to
sustain in the belief that it will reflect
credit on India itself, and to which the
present movie adheres slavishly), was until
fifty not ill-disposed to war at all. As I
have already noted, in three wars, no
sooner had the bugles sounded than
Gandhi not only gave his support, but was
clamoring for arms. To form new
regiments! To fight! To destroy the
enemies of the empire! Regular Indian
army units fought in both the Boer War
and World War I, but this was not enough
for Gandhi. He wanted to raise new troops,
even, in the case of the Boer and Kaffir
Wars, from the tiny Indian colony in South
Africa. British military authorities thought
it not really worth the trouble to train
such a small body of Indians as soldiers,
and were even resistant to training them as
an auxiliary medical corps ("stretcher
bearers"), but finally yielded to Gandhi's
relentless importuning. As first instructed,
the Indian Volunteer Corps was not
supposed actually to go into combat, but
Gandhi, adamant, led his Indian volunteers

into the thick of battle. When the British commanding officer was mortally wounded during an engagement in the Kaffir War, Gandhi—though his corps' deputy commander—carried the officer's stretcher himself from the battlefield and for miles over the sun-baked veldt. The British empire's War Medal did not have its name for nothing, and it was generally earned.

ANYONE who wants to wade through Gandhi's endless ruminations about *himsa* and *ahimsa* (violence and nonviolence) is welcome to do so, but it is impossible for the skeptical reader to avoid the conclusion—let us say in 1920, when *swaraj* (home rule) was all the rage and Gandhi's inner voice started telling him that *ahimsa* was the thing—that this inner voice knew what it was talking about. By this I mean that, though Gandhi talked with the tongue of Hindu gods and sacred scriptures, his inner voice had a strong sense of expediency. Britain, if only comparatively speaking, was a moral nation, and nonviolent civil disobedience was plainly the best and most effective way of achieving Indian independence. Skeptics might also not be surprised to learn that as independence approached, Gandhi's inner voice began to change its tune. It has been reported that Gandhi "half-welcomed" the civil war that broke out in the last days. Even a fratricidal "bloodbath" (Gandhi's word) would be preferable to the British.

And suddenly Gandhi began endorsing violence left, right, and center. During the fearsome rioting in Calcutta he gave his approval to men "using violence in a moral cause." How could he tell them that violence was wrong, he asked, "unless I demonstrate that nonviolence is more effective?" He blessed the Nawab of Maler Kotla when he gave orders to shoot ten Muslims for every Hindu killed in his state. He sang the praises of Subhas Chandra Bose, who, sponsored by first the Nazis and then the Japanese, organized in Singapore an Indian National Army with which he hoped to conquer India with Japanese support, establishing a

totalitarian dictatorship. Meanwhile, after
independence in 1947, the armies of the
India that Gandhi had created immediately
marched into battle, incorporating the
state of Hyderabad by force and making
war in Kashmir on secessionist Pakistan.
When Gandhi was assassinated by a Hindu
extremist in January 1948 he was honored
by the new state with a vast military
funeral—in my view by no means
inapposite.

BUT it is not widely realized (nor will this
film tell you) how much violence was
associated with Gandhi's so-called
"nonviolent" movement from the very
beginning. India's Nobel Prize-winning
poet, Rabindranath Tagore, had sensed a
strong current of nihilism in Gandhi
almost from his first days, and as early as
1920 wrote of Gandhi's "fierce joy of
annihilation," which Tagore feared would
lead India into hideous orgies of
devastation—which ultimately proved to be
the case. Robert Payne has said that there
was unquestionably an "unhealthy

atmosphere" among many of Gandhi's fanatic followers, and that Gandhi's habit of going to the edge of violence and then suddenly retreating was fraught with danger. "In matters of conscience I am uncompromising," proclaimed Gandhi proudly. "Nobody can make me yield." The judgment of Tagore was categorical. Much as he might revere Gandhi as a holy man, he quite detested him as a politician and considered that his campaigns were almost always so close to violence that it was utterly disingenuous to call them nonviolent.

For every *satyagraha* true believer, moreover, sworn not to harm the adversary or even to lift a finger in his own defense, there were sometimes thousands of incensed freebooters and skirmishers bound by no such vow. Gandhi, to be fair, was aware of this, and nominally deplored it—but with nothing like the consistency shown in the movie. The film leads the audience to believe that Gandhi's first "fast unto death," for example, was in protest against an act of barbarous violence, the slaughter by an Indian crowd of a detachment of police constables. But in actual fact Gandhi reserved this "ultimate weapon" of his to interdict a 1931 British proposal to grant Untouchables a "separate electorate" in the Indian national legislature—in effect a kind of affirmative-action program for Untouchables. For reasons I have not been able to decrypt, Gandhi was dead set against the project, but I confess it is another scene I would like to have seen in the movie: Gandhi almost starving himself to death to block affirmative action for Untouchables.

From what I have been able to decipher, Gandhi's main preoccupation in this particular struggle was not even the British. Benefiting from the immense publicity, he wanted to induce Hindus, overnight, ecstatically, and without any of these British legalisms, to "open their hearts" to Untouchables. For a whole week Hindu India was caught up in a joyous delirium. No more would the Untouchables be scavengers and sweepers! No more would they be banned from Hindu temples! No more would they pollute at sixty-four feet! It lasted just a week. Then the temple doors swung shut again, and all was as before. Meanwhile, on the passionate subject of *swaraj*, Gandhi was crying, "I would not flinch from sacrificing a million lives for India's liberty!" The million Indian lives were indeed sacrificed, and in full. They fell, however, not to the bullets of British soldiers but to the knives and clubs of their fellow Indians in savage butcheries when the British finally withdrew.

ALTHOUGH the movie sneers at this reasoning as being the flimsiest of pretexts, I cannot imagine an impartial person studying the subject without concluding that concern for Indian religious minorities was one of the principal reasons Britain stayed in India as long as it did. When it finally withdrew, blood-maddened mobs surged through the streets from one end of India to the other, the majority group in each area, Hindu or

Muslim, slaughtering the defenseless minority without mercy in one of the most hideous periods of carnage of modern history.

A comparison is in order. At the famous Amritsar massacre of 1919, shot in elaborate and loving detail in the present movie and treated by post-independence Indian historians as if it were Auschwitz, Ghurka troops under the command of a British officer, General Dyer, fired into an unarmed crowd of Indians defying a ban and demonstrating for Indian independence. The crowd contained women and children; 379 persons died; it was all quite horrible. Dyer was court-martialed and cashiered, but the incident lay heavily on British consciences for the next three decades, producing a severe inhibiting effect. Never again would the British empire commit another Amritsar, anywhere.

As soon as the oppressive British were gone, however, the Indians—gentle, tolerant people that they are—gave themselves over to an orgy of bloodletting.

The Gandhi Nobody Knows

Trained troops did not pick off targets at a distance with Enfield rifles. Blood-crazed Hindus, or Muslims, ran through the streets with knives, beheading babies, stabbing women, old people. Interestingly, our movie shows none of this on camera (the oldest way of stacking the deck in Hollywood). All we see is the aged Gandhi, grieving, and of course fasting, at these terrible reports of riots. And, naturally, the film doesn't whisper a clue as to the total number of dead, which might spoil the mood somehow. The fact is that we will never know how many Indians were murdered by other Indians during the country's Independence Massacres, but almost all serious studies place the figure over a million, and some, such as Payne's sources, go to *four million*. So, for those who like round numbers, the British killed some four hundred seditious colonials at Amritsar and the name Amritsar lives in infamy, while Indians may have killed some four million of their own countrymen for no other reason than that they were of a different religious faith and people think

their great leader would make an
inspirational subject for a movie. *Ahimsa,*
as can be seen, then, had an absolutely
tremendous moral effect when used against
Britain, but not only would it not have
worked against Nazi Germany (the most
obvious reproach, and of course quite
true), but, the crowning irony, it had
virtually no effect whatever when Gandhi
tried to bring it into play against violent
Indians.

Despite this at best patchy record, the
film-makers have gone to great lengths to
imply that this same principle of *ahimsa*—
presented in the movie as the purest form
of pacifism—is universally effective,
yesterday, today, here, there, everywhere.
We hear no talk from Gandhi of war
sometimes being a "necessary evil," but
only him announcing—and more than
once—"An eye for an eye makes the whole
world blind." In a scene very near the end
of the movie, we hear Gandhi say, as if
after deep reflection: "Tyrants and
murderers can seem invincible at the time,
but in the end they always fall. Think of it.

The Gandhi Nobody Knows

Always." During the last scene of the
movie, following the assassination,
Margaret Bourke-White is keening over the
death of the Great Soul with an English
admiral's daughter named Madeleine
Slade, in whose bowel movements Gandhi
took the deepest interest (see their
correspondence), and Miss Slade remarks
incredulously that Gandhi felt that he had
failed. They are then both incredulous for
a moment, after which Miss Slade observes
mournfully, "When we most needed it
[presumably meaning during World War
II], he offered the world a way out of
madness. But the world didn't see it." Then
we hear once again the assassin's shots,
Gandhi's "Oh, God," and last, in case we
missed them the first time, Gandhi's words
(over the shimmering waters of the
Ganges?): "Tyrants and murderers can
seem invincible at the time, but in the end
they always fall. Think of it. Always." This
is the end of the picture.

Now, as it happens, I have been thinking
about tyrants and murderers for some

time. But the fact that in the end they always fall has never given me much comfort, partly because, not being a Hindu and not expecting reincarnation after reincarnation, I am simply not prepared to wait them out. It always occurs to me that, while I am waiting around for them to fall, they might do something mean to me, like fling me into a gas oven or send me off to a Gulag. Unlike a Hindu and not worshiping stasis, I am also given to wondering who is to bring these murderers and tyrants down, it being all too risky a process to wait for them and the regimes they establish simply to die of old age. The fact that a few reincarnations from now they will all have turned to dust somehow does not seem to suggest a rational strategy for dealing with the problem.

Since the movie's Madeleine Slade specifically invites us to revere the "way out of madness" that Gandhi offered the world at the time of World War II, I am under the embarrassing obligation of recording exactly what courses of action the Great Soul recommended to the various parties involved in that crisis. For Gandhi was never stinting in his advice. Indeed, the less he knew about a subject, the less he stinted.

I am aware that for many not privileged to have visited the former British Raj, the names Gujarat, Rajasthan, and Deccan are simply words. But other names, such as Germany, Poland, Czechoslovakia, somehow have a harder profile. The term "Jew," also, has a reasonably hard profile, and I feel all Jews sitting emotionally at the movie *Gandhi* should be apprised of the advice that the Mahatma offered their coreligionists when faced with the Nazi peril: they should commit collective suicide. If only the Jews of Germany had the good sense to offer their throats willingly to the Nazi butchers' knives and throw themselves into the sea from cliffs they would arouse world public opinion, Gandhi was convinced, and their moral triumph would be remembered for "ages to come." If they would only pray for Hitler (as their throats were cut, presumably), they would leave a "rich heritage to

mankind." Although Gandhi had known
Jews from his earliest days in South
Africa—where his three staunchest white
supporters were Jews, every one—he
disapproved of how rarely they loved their
enemies. And he never repented of his
recommendation of collective suicide. Even
after the war, when the full extent of the
Holocaust was revealed, Gandhi told Louis
Fischer, one of his biographers, that the
Jews died anyway, didn't they? They might
as well have died significantly.

Gandhi's views on the European crisis
were not entirely consistent. He vigorously
opposed Munich, distrusting Chamberlain.
"Europe has sold her soul for the sake of a
seven days' earthly existence," he declared.
"The peace that Europe gained at Munich
is a triumph of violence." But when the
Germans moved into the Bohemian
heartland, he was back to urging
nonviolent resistance, exhorting the Czechs
to go forth, unarmed, against the
Wehrmacht, *perishing gloriously*—
collective suicide again. He had Madeleine
Slade draw up two letters to President

Eduard Beneš of Czechoslovakia, instructing him on the proper conduct of Czechoslovak *satyagrahi* when facing the Nazis.

When Hitler attacked Poland, however, Gandhi suddenly endorsed the Polish army's military resistance, calling it "almost nonviolent." (If this sounds like double-talk, I can only urge readers to read Gandhi.) He seemed at this point to have a rather low opinion of Hitler, but when Germany's panzer divisions turned west, Allied armies collapsed under the ferocious onslaught, and British ships were streaming across the Straits of Dover from Dunkirk, he wrote furiously to the Viceroy of India: "This manslaughter must be stopped. You are losing; if you persist, it will only result in greater bloodshed. Hitler is not a bad man. . . ."

Gandhi also wrote an open letter to the British people, passionately urging them to surrender and accept whatever fate Hitler had prepared for them. "Let them take possession of your beautiful island with your many beautiful buildings. You will

give all these, but neither your souls, nor
your minds." Since none of this had the
intended effect, Gandhi, the following year,
addressed an open letter to the prince of
darkness himself, Adolf Hitler.

THE scene must be pictured. In late
December 1941, Hitler stood at the
pinnacle of his might. His armies,
undefeated—anywhere—ruled Europe from
the English Channel to the Volga. Rommel
had entered Egypt. The Japanese had
reached Singapore. The U.S. Pacific Fleet
lay at the bottom of Pearl Harbor. At this
superbly chosen moment, Mahatma Gandhi
attempted to convert Adolf Hitler to the
ways of nonviolence. "Dear Friend," the
letter begins, and proceeds to a heartfelt
appeal to the Führer to embrace all
mankind "irrespective of race, color, or
creed." Every admirer of the film *Gandhi*
should be compelled to read this letter.
Surprisingly, it is not known to have had
any deep impact on Hitler. Gandhi was no
doubt disappointed. He moped about,
really quite depressed, but still knew he

was right. When the Japanese, having cut their way through Burma, threatened India, Gandhi's strategy was to let them occupy as much of India as they liked and then to "make them feel unwanted." His way of helping his British "friends" was, at one of the worst points of the war, to launch massive civil disobedience campaigns against them, paralyzing some of their efforts to defend India from the Japanese.

Here, then, is your leader, O followers of Gandhi: a man who thought Hitler's heart would be melted by an appeal to forget race, color, and creed, and who was sure the feelings of the Japanese would be hurt if they sensed themselves unwanted. As world-class statesmen go, it is not a very good record. Madeleine Slade was right, I suppose. The world certainly didn't listen to Gandhi. Nor, for that matter, has the modern government of India listened to Gandhi. Although all Indian politicians of all political parties claim to be Gandhians, India has blithely fought three wars against Pakistan, one against China, and

The Gandhi Nobody Knows

even invaded and seized tiny, helpless Goa,
and all without a whisper of a shadow of a
thought of *ahimsa*. And of course India
now has atomic weapons, a *satyagraha*
technique if ever there was one.

83

I AM SURE that almost everyone who sees the movie *Gandhi* is aware that, from a religious point of view, the Mahatma was something called a "Hindu"—but I do not think one in a thousand has the dimmest notion of the fundamental beliefs of the Hindu religion. The simplest example is Gandhi's use of the word "God," which, for members of the great Western religions— Christianity, Judaism, and Islam, all interrelated—means a personal god, a godhead. But when Gandhi said "God" in speaking English, he was merely translating from Gujarati or Hindi, and from the Hindu culture. Gandhi, in fact, simply did not believe in a personal God, and wrote in so many words, "God is not a person . . . but a force; the undefinable mysterious Power that pervades everything; a living Power that is Love. . . ." And Gandhi's very favorite definition of God, repeated many thousands of times, was, "God is Truth," which reduces God to some kind of abstract principle.

Like all Hindus, Gandhi also believed in the "Great Oneness," according to which everything is part of God, meaning not just you and me and everyone else, but every living creature, every dead creature, every plant, the pitcher of milk, the milk in the pitcher, the tumbler into which the milk is poured. . . . After all of which, he could suddenly pop up with a declaration that God is "the Maker, the Law-Giver, a jealous Lord," phrases he had probably picked up in the Bible and, with Hindu fluidity, felt he could throw in so as to embrace even more of the Great Oneness. So when Gandhi said, "I am a Hindu and a Muslim and a Christian and a Jew," it was (from a Western standpoint) Hindu double-talk. Hindu holy men, some of them reformers like Gandhi, have actually even "converted" to Islam, then Christianity, or whatever, to worship different "aspects" of the Great Oneness, before reconverting to Hinduism. Now for Christians, fastidious in matters of doctrine, a man who converts to Islam is an apostate (or vice versa), but a Hindu is a Hindu is a Hindu. The better to experience the Great Oneness, many Hindu holy men feel they should be women as well as men, and one quite famous one even claimed he could menstruate (I will spare the reader the details).

IN THIS ecumenical age, it is extremely hard to shake Westerners loose from the notion that the devout of all religions, after all, worship "the one God." But Gandhi did not worship the one God. He did not worship the God of mercy. He did not worship the God of forgiveness. And this for the simple reason that the concepts of mercy and forgiveness are absent from Hinduism. In Hinduism, men do not pray to God for forgiveness, and a man's sins are never forgiven—indeed, there is no one out there to do the forgiving. In your next life you may be born someone higher up the caste scale, but in this life there is no hope. For Gandhi, a true Hindu, did not believe in man's immortal soul. He believed with every ounce of his being in *karma,* a series, perhaps a long series, of reincarnations, and at the end, with great good fortune: *mukti,* liberation from suffering and the necessity of rebirth, nothingness. Gandhi once wrote to Tolstoy (of all people) that reincarnation explained "reasonably the many mysteries of life." So if Hindus today still treat an Untouchable as barely human, this is thought to be perfectly right and fitting because of his actions in earlier lives. As can be seen, Hinduism, by its very theology, with its sacred triad of *karma,* reincarnation, and caste (with caste an absolutely indispensable part of the system) offers the most complacent justification of inhumanity of any of the world's great religious faiths.

Gandhi, needless to say, was a Hindu reformer, one of many. Until well into his fifties, however, he accepted the caste system *in toto* as the "natural order of society," promoting control and discipline and sanctioned by his religion. Later, in bursts of zeal, he favored moderating it in a number of ways. But he stuck by the basic *varna* system (the four main caste groupings plus the Untouchables) until the end of his days, insisting that a man's position and occupation should be determined essentially by birth. Gandhi favored milder treatment of Untouchables, renaming them Harijans, "children of God," but a Harijan was still a Harijan. Perhaps because his frenzies of compassion were so extreme (no, no, *he* would clean the *Harijan's* latrine), Hindu reverence for him as a holy man became immense, but his prescriptions were rarely followed. Industrialization and modernization have introduced new occupations and sizable social and political changes in India, but the caste system has dexterously adapted and remains largely intact today. The Sudras still labor. The sweepers still sweep. Max Weber, in his *The Religion of India,* after quoting the last line of the *Communist Manifesto*, suggests somewhat sardonically that low-caste Hindus, too, have "nothing to lose but their chains," that they, too, have "a world to win"—the only problem being that they have to die first and get born again, higher, it is to be hoped, in the immutable system of caste. Hinduism in general, wrote Weber, "is characterized by a dread of the magical evil of innovation." Its very essence is to guarantee stasis.

In addition to its literally thousands of castes and sub-castes, Hinduism has countless sects, with discordant rites and beliefs. It has no clear ecclesiastical organization and no universal body of doctrine. What I have described above is your standard, no-frills Hindu, of which in many ways Gandhi was an excellent example. With the reader's permission I will skip over the Upanishads, Vedanta, Yoga, the Puranas, Tantra, Bhakti, the *Bhagavad-Gita* (which contains theistic elements), Brahma, Vishnu, Shiva, and the terrible Kali or Durga, to concentrate on those central beliefs that most motivated Gandhi's behavior as a public figure.

IT SHOULD be plain by now that there is much in the Hindu culture that is distasteful to the Western mind, and consequently is largely unknown in the West—not because Hindus do not go on and on about these subjects, but because a Western squeamishness usually prevents these preoccupations from reaching print (not to mention film). When Gandhi attended his first Indian National Congress he was most distressed at seeing the Hindus—not laborers but high-caste Hindus, civic leaders—defecating all over the place, as if to pay attention to where the feces fell was somehow unclean. (For, as V. S. Naipaul puts it, in a twisted Hindu way it is *unclean to clean*. It is unclean even to notice. "It was the business of the sweepers to remove excrement, and until the sweepers came, people were content to live in the midst of their own excrement.") Gandhi exhorted Indians endlessly on the subject, saying that sanitation was the first

need of India, but he retained an obvious
obsession with excreta, gleefully designing
latrines and latrine drills for all hands at
the ashram, and, all in all, what with
giving and taking enemas, and his public
bowel movements, and his deep concern
with everyone else's bowel movements
(much correspondence), and endless dietary
experiments *as a function* of bowel
movements, he devoted a rather large share
of his life to the matter. Despite his
constant campaigning for sanitation, it is
hard to believe that Gandhi was not
permanently marked by what Arthur
Koestler terms the Hindu "morbid
infatuation with filth," and what V. S.
Naipaul goes as far as to call the Indian
"deification of filth." (Decades later,
Krishna Menon, a Gandhian and one-time
Indian Defense Minister, was still
fortifying his sanctity by drinking a daily
glass of urine.)

But even more important, because it is
dealt with in the movie directly—if of
course dishonestly—is Gandhi's parallel
obsession with *brahmacharya,* or sexual

chastity. There is a scene late in the film in which Margaret Bourke-White (again!) asks Gandhi's wife if he has ever broken his vow of chastity, taken, at that time, about forty years before. Gandhi's wife, by now a sweet old lady, answers wistfully, with a pathetic little note of hope, "Not yet." What lies behind this adorable scene is the following: Gandhi held as one of his most profound beliefs (a fundamental doctrine of Hindu medicine) that a man, as a matter of the utmost importance, must conserve his *bindu,* or seminal fluid. Koestler (in *The Lotus and the Robot*) gives a succinct account of this belief, widespread among orthodox Hindus: "A man's vital energy is concentrated in his seminal fluid, and this is stored in a cavity in the skull. It is the most precious substance in the body . . an elixir of life both in the physical and mystical sense, distilled from the blood. . . . A large store of *bindu* of pure quality guarantees health, longevity, and supernatural powers. . . . Conversely, every loss of it is a physical and spiritual impoverishment." Gandhi himself said in so many words, "A man who is unchaste loses stamina, becomes emasculated and cowardly, while in the chaste man secretions [semen] are sublimated into a vital force pervading his whole being." And again, still Gandhi: "Ability to retain and assimilate the vital liquid is a matter of long training. When properly conserved it is transmuted into matchless energy and strength." Most male Hindus go ahead and have sexual relations anyway, of course, but the belief in the value of *bindu* leaves the whole culture in what many observers have called a permanent state of "semen anxiety." When Gandhi once had a nocturnal emission he almost had a nervous breakdown.

Gandhi was a truly fanatical opponent of sex for pleasure, and worked it out carefully that a married couple should be allowed to have sex three or four times *in a lifetime,* merely to have children, and favored embodying this restriction in the law of the land. The sexual-gratification wing of the present-day feminist movement would find little to attract them in

The Gandhi Nobody Knows

Gandhi's doctrine, since in all his seventy-nine years it never crossed his mind once that there could be anything enjoyable in sex for women, and he was constantly enjoining Indian women to deny themselves to men, to refuse to let their husbands "abuse" them. Gandhi had been married at thirteen, and when he took his vow of chastity, after twenty-four years of sexual activity, he ordered his two oldest sons, both young men, to be totally chaste as well.

BUT Gandhi's monstrous behavior to his own family is notorious. He denied his sons education—to which he was bitterly hostile. His wife remained illiterate. Once when she was very sick, hemorrhaging badly, and seemed to be dying, he wrote to her from jail icily:

> My struggle is not merely political. It is religious and therefore quite pure. It does not matter much whether one dies in it or lives. I hope and expect that you will also think likewise and not be unhappy.

To die, that is. On another occasion he
wrote, speaking about her:

> I simply cannot bear to look at Ba's
> face. The expression is often like that
> on the face of a meek cow and gives
> one the feeling, as a cow occasionally
> does, that in her own dumb manner
> she is saying something. I see, too, that
> there is selfishness in this suffering of
> hers. .

And in the end he let her die, as I have
said, rather than allow British doctors to
give her a shot of penicillin (while his
inner voice told him that it would be all
right for him to take quinine). He
disowned his oldest son, Harilal, for
wishing to marry. He banished his second
son for giving his struggling older brother
a small sum of money. Harilal grew quite
wild with rage against his father, attacked
him in print, converted to Islam, took to
women, drink, and died an alcoholic in
1948. The Mahatma attacked him right
back in his pious way, proclaiming

modestly in an open letter in *Young India,* "Men may be good, not necessarily their children."

IF THE reader thinks I have delivered unduly harsh judgments on India and Hindu civilization, I can refer him to *An Area of Darkness* and *India: A Wounded Civilization,* two quite brilliant books on India by V. S. Naipaul, a Hindu, and a Brahmin, born in Trinidad. In the second, the more discursive, Naipaul writes that India

> has little to offer the world except its Gandhian concept of holy poverty and the recurring crooked comedy of its holy men, and . . . is now dependent in every practical way on other, imperfectly understood civilizations.

Hinduism, Naipaul writes,

> has given men no idea of a contract with other men, no idea of the state. It has enslaved one quarter of the

population [the Untouchables] and
always has left the whole fragmented
and vulnerable. Its philosophy of
withdrawal has diminished men
intellectually and not equipped them
to respond to challenge; it has stifled
growth. So that again and again in
India history has repeated itself:
vulnerability, defeat, withdrawal

Indians, Naipaul says, have no historical
notion of the past.

Through centuries of conquest the
civilization declined into an apparatus
for survival, turning away from the
mind . . . and creativity . . . stripping
itself down, like all decaying
civilizations, to its magical practices
and imprisoning social forms.

He adds later,

No government can survive on
Gandhian fantasy; and the spirituality,
the solace of a conquered people,

which Gandhi turned into a form of
national assertion, has soured more
obviously into the nihilism that it
always was.

Naipaul condemns India again and again
for its "intellectual parasitism," its
"intellectual vacuum," its "emptiness," the
"blankness of its decayed civilization."

Indian poverty is more dehumanizing
than any machine; and, more than in
any machine civilization, men in India
are units, locked up in the straitest
obedence by their idea of their
dharma. . . . The blight of caste is not
only untouchability and the
consequent deification in India of
filth; the blight, in an India that tries
to grow, is also the overall obedience it
imposes, . . . the diminishing of
adventurousness, the pushing away
from men of individuality and the
possibility of excellence.

Although Naipaul blames Gandhi as well
as India itself for the country's failure to

develop an "ideology" adequate for the modern world, he grants him one or two magnificent moments—always, it should be noted, when responding to "other civilizations." For Gandhi, Naipaul remarks pointedly, had matured in alien societies: Britain and South Africa. With age, back in India, he seemed from his autobiography to be headed for "lunacy," says Naipaul, and was only rescued by external events, his reactions to which were determined in part by *"his experience of the democratic ways of South Africa"* [my emphasis]. For it is one of the enduring ironies of Gandhi's story that it was in South Africa—*South Africa*—a country in which he became far more deeply involved than he had been in Britain, that Gandhi caught a warped glimmer of that strange institution of which he would never have seen even a reflection within Hindu society: democracy.

ANOTHER of Gandhi's most powerful obsessions (to which the movie alludes in such a syrupy and misleading manner that it would be quite impossible for the audience to understand it) was his visceral hatred of the modern, industrial world. He even said, more than once, that he actually wouldn't mind if the British remained in India, to police it, conduct foreign policy, and such trivia, if it would only take away its factories and railways. And Gandhi hated, not just factories and railways, but also the telegraph, the telephone, the radio, the airplane. He happened to be in England when Louis Blériot, the great French aviation pioneer, first flew the English Channel—an event which at the time stirred as much excitement as Lindbergh's later flight across the Atlantic—and Gandhi was in a positive fury that giant crowds were acclaiming such an insignificant event. He used the telegraph extensively himself, of course, and later would broadcast daily over All-India Radio during his highly publicized fasts, but consistency was never Gandhi's strong suit.

The Gandhi Nobody Knows

Gandhi's view of the good society, about which he wrote *ad nauseam,* was an Arcadian vision set far in India's past. It was the pristine Indian village, where, with all diabolical machinery and technology abolished—and with them all unhappiness—contented villagers would hand-spin their own yarn, hand-weave their own cloth, serenely follow their bullocks in the fields, tranquilly prodding them in the anus in the time-hallowed Hindu way. This was why Gandhi taught himself to spin, and why all the devout Gandhians, like monkeys, spun also. This was Gandhi's program. Since he said it several thousand times, we have no choice but to believe that he sincerely desired the destruction of modern technology and industry and the return of India to the way of life of an idyllic (and quite likely nonexistent) past. And yet this same Mahatma Gandhi hand-picked as the first Prime Minister of an independent India Pandit Nehru, who was committed to a policy of industrialization and for whom

the last word in the politico-economic
organization of the state was (and
remained) Beatrice Webb.

WHAT are we to make of this Gandhi? We
are dealing with two strangenesses here,
Indians and Gandhi himself. The plain fact
is that both Indian leaders and the Indian
people ignored Gandhi's precepts almost as
thoroughly as did Hitler. They ignored him
on sexual abstinence. They ignored his
modifications of the caste system. They
ignored him on the evils of modern
industry, the radio, the telephone. They
ignored him on education. They ignored
his appeals for national union, the former
British Raj splitting into a Muslim
Pakistan and a Hindu India. No one sought
a return to the Arcadian Indian village of
antiquity. They ignored him, above all, on
ahimsa, nonviolence. There was always a
small number of exalted *satyagrahi* who,
martyrs, would march into the constables'
truncheons, but one of the things that
alarmed the British—as Tagore indicated—
was the explosions of violence that

accompanied all this alleged nonviolence. Naipaul writes that with independence India discovered again that it was "cruel and horribly violent." Jaya Prakash Narayan, the late opposition leader, once admitted, "We often behave like animals. . . . We are more likely than not to become aggressive, wild, violent. We kill and burn and loot. . . ."

Why, then, did the Hindu masses so honor this Mahatma, almost all of whose most cherished beliefs they so pointedly ignored, even during his lifetime? For Hindus, the question is not really so puzzling. Gandhi, for them, after all, was a Mahatma, a holy man. He was a symbol of sanctity, not a guide to conduct. Hinduism has a long history of holy men who, traditionally, do not offer themselves up to the public as models of general behavior but withdraw from the world, often into an ashram, to pursue their sanctity in private, a practice which all Hindus honor, if few emulate. The true oddity is that Gandhi, this holy man, having drawn from British sources his notions of nationalism

and democracy, also absorbed from the
British his model of virtue in public life.
He was a historical original, a Hindu holy
man that a British model of public service
and dazzling advances in mass
communications thrust out into the world,
to become a great moral leader and the
"father of his country."

SOME Indians feel that after the early
1930s, Gandhi, although by now world-
famous, was in fact in sharp decline. Did
he at least "get the British out of India"?
Some say no. India, in the last days of the
British Raj, was already largely governed
by Indians (a fact one would never suspect
from this movie), and it is a common view
that without this irrational, wildly erratic
holy man the transition to full
independence might have gone both more
smoothly and more swiftly. There is much
evidence that in his last years Gandhi was
in a kind of spiritual retreat and, with all
his endless praying and fasting, was no
longer pursuing (the very words seem
strange in a Hindu context) "the public

good." What he was pursuing, in a strict reversion to Hindu tradition, was his personal holiness. In earlier days he had scoffed at the title accorded him, Mahatma (literally "great soul"). But toward the end, during the hideous paroxysms that accompanied independence, with some of the most unspeakable massacres taking place in Calcutta, he declared, "And if . . . the whole of Calcutta swims in blood, it will not dismay me. For it will be a willing offering of innocent blood." And in his last days, after there had already been one attempt on his life, he was heard to say, "*I am a true Mahatma.*"

We can only wonder, furthermore, at a public figure who lectures half his life about the necessity of abolishing modern industry and returning India to its ancient primitiveness, and then picks a Fabian socialist, already drawing up Five-Year Plans, as the country's first Prime Minister. Audacious as it may seem to contest the views of such heavy thinkers as Margaret Bourke-White, Ralph Nader, and J. K. Galbraith (who found the film's Gandhi "true to the original" and endorsed the movie wholeheartedly), we have a right to reservations about such a figure as a public man.

I should not be surprised if Gandhi's greatest real humanitarian achievement was an improvement in the treatment of Untouchables—an area where his efforts were not only assiduous, but actually bore fruit. In this, of course, he ranks well behind the British, who abolished *suttee*— over ferocious Hindu opposition—in 1829. The ritual immolation by fire of widows on their husbands' funeral pyres, *suttee* had the full sanction of the Hindu religion, although it might perhaps be wrong to overrate its importance. Scholars remind us that it was never universal, only "usual." And there was, after all, a rather extensive range of choice. In southern India the widow was flung into her husband's fire-pit. In the valley of the Ganges she was placed on the pyre when it was already aflame. In western India, she supported the head of the corpse with her right hand, while, torch in her left, she was

allowed the honor of setting the whole
thing on fire herself. In the north, where
perhaps women were more impious, the
widow's body was constrained on the
burning pyre by long poles pressed down
by her relatives, just in case, screaming in
terror and choking and burning to death,
she might forget her *dharma.* So, yes,
ladies, members of the National Council of
Churches, believers in the one God,
mourners for that holy India before it was
despoiled by those brutish British,
remember *suttee,* that interesting, exotic
practice in which Hindus, over the
centuries, burned to death countless
millions of helpless women in a spirit of
pious devotion, crying for all I know, *Hai
Rama! Hai Rama!*

I WOULD like to conclude with some observations on two Englishmen, Madeleine Slade, the daughter of a British admiral, and Sir Richard Attenborough, the producer, director, and spiritual godfather of the film, *Gandhi*. Miss Slade was a jewel in Gandhi's crown—a member of the British ruling class, as she was, turned fervent disciple of this Indian Mahatma. She is played in the film by Geraldine James with nobility, dignity, and a beatific manner quite up to the level of Candice Bergen, and perhaps even the Virgin Mary. I learn from Ved Mehta's *Mahatma Gandhi and his Apostles*, however, that Miss Slade had another master before Gandhi. In about 1917, when she was fifteen, she made contact with the spirit of Beethoven by listening to his sonatas on a player piano. "I threw myself down on my knees in the seclusion of my room," she wrote in her autobiography, "and prayed, *really* prayed to God for the first time in my life: 'Why have I been born over a century too late? Why hast Thou given me realization of him and yet put all these years in between?'"

After World War I, still seeking how best to serve Beethoven, Miss Slade felt an "infinite longing" when she visited his birthplace and grave, and, finally, at the age of thirty-two, caught up with Romain Rolland, who had partly based his renowned *Jean Christophe* on the composer. But Rolland had written a new book now, about a man called Gandhi, "another Christ," and before long Miss Slade was quite literally falling on her knees before the Mahatma in India, "conscious of nothing but a sense of light." Although one would never guess this from the film, she soon (to quote Mehta's impression) began "to get on Gandhi's nerves," and he took every pretext to keep her away from him, in other ashrams, and working in schools and villages in other parts of India. She complained to Gandhi in letters about discrimination against her by orthodox Hindus, who expected her to live in rags and vile quarters during menstruation, considering her unclean and virtually untouchable. Gandhi wrote back, agreeing that women should not be treated like that, but adding that she should accept it all with grace and cheerfulness, "without thinking that the orthodox party is in any way unreasonable." (This is as good an example as any of Gandhi's coherence, even in his prime. Women should not be treated like that, but the people who treated them that way were in no way unreasonable.)

Some years after Gandhi's death, Miss Slade rediscovered Beethoven, becoming conscious again "of the realization of my true self. For a while I remained lost in the world of the spirit. . . ." She soon returned to Europe and serving Beethoven, her "true calling." When Mehta finally found her in

The Gandhi Nobody Knows

Vienna, she told him, "Please don't ask me any more about Bapu [Gandhi]. I now belong to van Beethoven. In matters of the spirit, there is always a call." A polite description of Madeleine Slade is that she was an extreme eccentric. In the vernacular, she was slightly cracked.

Sir Richard Attenborough, however, isn't cracked at all. The only puzzle is how he suddenly got to be a pacifist, a fact which his press releases now proclaim to the world. Attenborough trained as a pilot in the RAF in World War II, and was released briefly to the cinema, where he had already begun his career in Noël Coward's superpatriotic *In Which We Serve*. He then returned to active service, flying combat missions with the RAF. Richard Attenborough, in short—when Gandhi was pleading with the British to surrender to the Nazis, assuring them that "Hitler is not a bad man"—was fighting for his country. The Viceroy of India warned Gandhi grimly that "We are engaged in a struggle," and Attenborough played his part in that great struggle, and proudly, too, as far as I can tell. To my knowledge he has never had a *crise de conscience* on the matter, or announced that he was carried away by the war fever and that Britain really should have capitulated to the Nazis— which Gandhi would have had it do.

ALTHOUGH the present film is handsomely done in its way, no one has ever accused Attenborough of being excessively endowed with either acting or directing talent. In the 50s he was a popular young British entertainer, but his most singular gift appeared to be his entrepreneurial talent as a businessman, using his movie fees to launch successful London restaurants (at one time four), and other business ventures. At the present moment he is Chairman of the Board of Capital Radio (Britain's most successful commercial station), Goldcrest Films, the British Film Institute, and Deputy Chairman of the BBC's new Channel 4 television network. Like most members of the *nouveaux riches* on the rise, he has also reached out for symbols of respectability

and public service, and has assembled
quite a collection. He is a Trustee of the
Tate Gallery, Pro-Chancellor of Sussex
University, President of Britain's Muscular
Dystrophy Group, Chairman of the Actors'
Charitable Trust and, of course, Chairman
of the Royal Academy of Dramatic Art.
There may be even more, but this is a fair
sampling. In 1976, quite fittingly, he was
knighted, by a Labor government, but his
friends say he still insists on being called
"Dickie."

It is quite general today for members of
the professional classes, even when not
artistic types, to despise commerce and
feel that the state, the economy, and almost
everything else would be better and more
idealistically run by themselves rather
than these loutish businessmen. Sir Dickie,
however, being a highly successful
businessman himself, would hardly
entertain such an antipathy. But as he
scrambled his way to the heights perhaps
he found himself among high-minded
idealists, utopians, equalitarians, and
lovers of the oppressed. Now there are

those who think Sir Dickie converted to pacifism when Indira Gandhi handed him a check for several million dollars. But I do not believe this. I think Sir Dickie converted to pacifism out of idealism.

His pacifism, I confess, has been more than usually muddled. In 1968, after twenty-six years in the profession, he made his directorial debut with *Oh! What a Lovely War,* with its superb parody of Britain's jingoistic music-hall songs of the "Great War," World War I. Since I had the good fortune to see Joan Littlewood's original London stage production, which gave the work its entire style, I cannot think that Sir Dickie's contribution was unduly large. Like most commercially successful parodies—from Sandy Wilson's *The Boy Friend* to Broadway's *Superman, Dracula,* and *The Crucifier of Blood—Oh! What a Lovely War* depended on the audience's (if not Miss Littlewood's) retaining a substantial affection for the subject being parodied: in this case, a swaggering hyper-patriotism, which recalled days when the

empire was great. In any event, since Miss
Littlewood identified herself as a
Communist and since Communists, as far
as I know, are never pacifists, Sir Dickie's
case for the production's "pacifism" seems
stymied from the other angle as well.

Sir Dickie's next blow for pacifism was
Young Winston (1973), which, the new
publicity manual says, "explored how
Churchill's childhood traumas and lack of
parental affection became the spurs which
goaded him to . . . a position of great
power." One would think that a man who
once flew combat missions under the
orders of the great war leader—and who
seemingly wanted his country to win—
would thank God for childhood traumas
and lack of parental affection if such were
needed to provide a Churchill in the hour
of peril. But on pressed Sir Dickie, in the
year of his knighthood, with *A Bridge Too
Far,* the story of the futile World War II
assault on Arnhem, described by Sir
Dickie—now, at least—as "a further plea
for pacifism."

But does Sir Richard Attenborough

seriously think that, rather than go through what we did at Arnhem, we should have given in, let the Nazis be, and even—true pacifists—let them occupy Britain, Canada, the United States, contenting ourselves only with "making them feel unwanted"? At the level of idiocy to which discussions of war and peace have sunk in the West, every harebrained idealist who discovers that war is not a day at the beach seems to think he has found an irresistible argument for pacifism. Is Pearl Harbor an argument for pacifism? Bataan? Dunkirk? Dieppe? The Ardennes? Roland fell at Roncesvalles. Is the *Song of Roland* a pacifist epic? If so, why did William the Conqueror have it chanted to his men as they marched into battle at Hastings? Men proved their valor in defeat as well as in victory. Even Sergeant-Major Gandhi knew that. Up in the moral never-never land which Sir Dickie now inhabits, perhaps they think the Alamo led to a great wave of pacifism in Texas.

The Gandhi Nobody Knows

In a feat of sheer imbecility,
Attenborough has dedicated *Gandhi* to
Lord Mountbatten, who commanded the
Southeast Asian Theater during World War
II. Mountbatten, you might object, was
hardly a pacifist—but then again he was
murdered by Irish terrorists, which proves
how frightful all that sort of thing is, Sir
Dickie says, and how we must end it all by
imitating Gandhi. Not the Gandhi who
called for seas of innocent blood, you
understand, but the movie-Gandhi, the
nice one.

THE historical Gandhi's favorite mantra,
strange to tell, was *Do or Die* (he called it
literally that, a "mantra"). I think Sir
Dickie should reflect on this, because it
means, *dixit* Gandhi, that a man must be
prepared to die for what he believes in, for,
himsa or *ahimsa,* death is always there,
and in an ultimate test men who are not
prepared to face it lose. Gandhi was
erratic, irrational, tyrannical, obstinate. He
sometimes verged on lunacy. He believed in

a religion whose ideas I find somewhat repugnant. He worshipped cows. But I still say this: he was brave. He feared no one.

On a lower level of being, I have consequently given some thought to the proper mantra for spectators of the movie *Gandhi*. After much reflection, in homage to Ralph Nader, I have decided on *Caveat Emptor*, "buyer beware." Repeated many thousand times in a seat in the cinema it might with luck lead to *Om*, the Hindu dream of nothingness, the Ultimate Void.

RICHARD GRENIER

Richard Grenier hails from Boston and graduated from the United States Naval Academy. He served in the Atlantic and Pacific fleets, first in Europe then all over Asia, did graduate work at Harvard, and was then a Fulbright Scholar in Paris, where he studied at the Sorbonne and the Institute of Political Studies. He has had careers as a foreign correspondent (for the French, British, and American press), which has taken him all over the world, as a movie scriptwriter (he also acted in a major film of Jean-Luc Godard), and most recently as a hard-hitting intellectual and political critic in the pages of *The New York Times, The New Republic, The American Spectator, Commentary,* the *Wall Street Journal,* and *The Times* of London.

His novel on the Arab world, *The Marrakesh One-Two,* is being published by Houghton Mifflin simultaneously with *The Gandhi Nobody Knows,* and has already received high praise from *Publisher's Weekly, The New Republic,* and the *New York Times.*

SELECTED BIBLIOGRAPHY

Books on Gandhi:

Fischer, Louis. *The Life of Mahatma Gandhi.* New York: Harper and Bros., 1950.

Mehta, Ved. *Mahatma Gandhi and His Apostles.* New York: Viking, 1977.

Orwell, George. "Reflections on Gandhi." In *The Collected Essays, Journalism and Letters of George Orwell,* Vol. 4, edited by Sonia Orwell and Ian Angus, 463-70. New York: Harcourt Brace Jovanovich, 1968.

Payne, Robert. *The Life and Death of Mahatma Gandhi.* New York: E. P. Dutton, 1969.

Sheean, Vincent. *Lead, Kindly Light.* New York: Random House, 1949.

Sheean, Vincent. *Mahatma Gandhi.* New York: Alfred Knopf, 1955.

Books on India:

Koestler, Arthur. *The Lotus and the Robot.* New York: Macmillan, 1961.

Naipaul, V. S. *An Area of Darkness.* London: André Deutsch, 1964.

Naipaul, V. S. *India: A Wounded Civilization.* New York: Alfred Knopf, 1977.

Nossiter, Bernard D. *Soft State: A Newspaperman's Chronicle of India.* New York: Harper and Row, 1970.